My Hungry Vegan Temple
INTERNATIONAL

AISHA DE IRISH-HAMILTON

AuthorHouse™
1663 Liberty Drive
Bloomington, IN 47403
www.authorhouse.com
Phone: 1 (800) 839-8640

This book is printed on acid-free paper.

ISBN: 978-1-7283-4640-3 (sc)
ISBN: 978-1-7283-4641-0 (e)

Library of Congress Control Number: 2020903857

Print information available on the last page.

Published by AuthorHouse 02/28/2020

authorHOUSE

Me

Aisha De Irish

Aisha currently resides in the Sunshine State of Southwest Florida with her husband and three children. She grew up watching her father and uncles from both sides of her family cook some of the tastiest foods ever. One of her uncles owned a Jamaican restaurant in Bronx, New York. She spent lots of time watching him in the kitchen and being creative with many traditional dishes.

Feeling more than inspired, she made her parents' kitchen her laboratory. She experimented with any herbs, spices and oils that she could get her hands on. Her parents had tons of cookbooks in the home for as long as she could remember. It was exciting to prepare meals for her family.

When her parents were busy with work in order to provide for Aisha and her three younger siblings, friends and family always requested for Aisha to make some of their favorite foods for their gatherings and functions. As much as she enjoyed doing it, years passed before she gained the confidence to actually make something of her gift.

In 2013, she started her own catering business called "Island Sunset Catering". Her clientele grew slowly but surely. Although it did so, she wasn't seeing the fruits of her labor. She knew that something had to change for improvement. That very same year, she enrolled in culinary school at Lincoln Culinary School in Shelton, Connecticut. After two years, she graduated with high honors and acquired the necessary tools that she could carry with her forever.

She remains confident that the Most High will bless her in the near future with a successful restaurant that will promote great food and health. She plans to consistently close the restaurant to the public one day a week, and provide a full course meal to the hungry. She always finds it a blessing to be a blessing.

Contents

STARTERS

- Baked Pakora (Indian)
- Corn and Sea Weed Fritters (Bahamian)
- Carmelized Onions & Mushrooms on Baguettes (American/French)
- Hummus & Veggies (Middle Eastern)

Baked pakora w/ mango pineapple chutney

Baked Pakora

(Indian)

Ingredients (40-50 Count)

- Red Potato (1 Grated)
- Carrot (1 large grated)
- Cauliflower (3 cups diced)
- Onion (1 medium diced)
- Peas (½ cup frozen)
- Garlic (3 cloves crushed)
- Crushed Red Pepper Flakes (1 tsp)
- Cumin (2 tsp)

- Turmeric (1 tsp)
- Sea salt (2 tsp)
- Garam Masala (2 tsp)
- Chickpea Flour (2 cups)
- Baking Powder (1 tsp)
- Water (1 ¼ cup then ¼ cup again)
- Garlic Powder (1 tsp)

Method:

- Preheat oven to 500°
- Place parchment paper on Baking Sheet
- In a large bowl, mix all dry ingredients
- Stir in ¼ cup of water and stir. Batter should be thick, but if too thick, more water may be added but not to exceed another ¼ cup
- Mix in veggies
- Using a tablespoon, scoop batter and place on Baking Sheet one at a time being sure not to place too close together
- Bake for 8-10 minutes
- Flip and Bake another 8-10 minutes

Eat w/ Chutney or Ketchup as a Sauce

Bahamian corn fritters w/zesty coconut dipping sauce

Corn Fritters

(Bahamian)

Ingredients (3-5 count)

- All purpose Flour (¾ cup)
- Onion (½ medium and chopped)
- Celery (1/2 chopped fine)
- Red Bell pepper (¼ chopped)
- Corn (1 cup frozen)
- Garlic Powder (1 tbsp)
- Sea Salt (to taste)
- Black Pepper (1 tsp)
- Cayenne Pepper (1 tsp)
- Coconut Milk (½ cup)
- Vegetable oil (enough for frying)

Method

- In a bowl, combine all spices and flour mix
- Add coconut milk and mix again
- Heat oil medium to medium high heat in a pan or deep fryer
- Using a table spoon, scoop up batter one at a time and drop in hot oil
- Fry until golden brown on each side
- Drain on Paper towels

*Served w/ Zesty lime dip (recipe in last section)
*Optional to use a seaweed sheet(s) and crumble adding to the batter for a "sea like taste"

Carmelized Mushroom & Onions on Baguettes

(American/French)

Ingredients (6-8 servings)

- Baby Bella Mushrooms (3 cups sliced)
- Garlic (2 cloves chopped)
- Onion (1 large sliced thin)
- Soy sauce (½ tbsp..)
- White wine (¼ cup)
- Sea salt (to taste)
- Pepper (to taste)
- Olive oil (2 tbsp..)
- French Baguette (½ sliced ½ an inch thin)

* Parsley for garnishing*

Method

- In a pan over medium high heat, sauté onion and garlic until softened about 3 minutes in olive oil
- Add mushrooms and cook for another 10 minutes stirring a few times in between
- Add salt, pepper, wine and soy sauce and cook for another 3-5 minutes
- Place baguettes in oven directly on rack to desired crustiness without burning
- Place onions and mushrooms on each sliced baguette and garnish with parsley

Hummus w/ Veggies

(Middle Eastern)

Ingredients (10 servings)

- Lemon (Juice of 1)
- Sea salt (to taste)
- Garlic (1 clove minced)
- Garbanzo Beans/Chickpeas (16 oz. can drained and rinsed)
- Olive Oil (3 tbsp..)
- Cumin (¼ teaspoon)
- Red bell pepper (1 sliced)
- Celery (5 sliced diagonally in sticks)
- Kalamata Olives (1 cup)
- Carrots (3 sliced Diagonally)

Method

- In a food processor, blend together beans, garlic, olive oil, cumin, salt, and lemon juice until smooth
- Scrape down sides as needed and place in a dish to be served with vegetables

SOUPS

- Potato Soup (American)
- Callaloo & Okra Soup (Grenadian)
- Southwest Quinoa (American/Mexican)
- Creamy Tomato Basil (American)

Potato Soup

(American)

Ingredients (6 servings)

- Onion (1 large chopped)
- Carrot (2 peeled and sliced)
- Potatoes (Russet, peeled & chopped in medium chunks)
- Garlic (6 cloves minced)
- White pepper (to taste)
- Sea salt (to taste)
- Smoked Paprika (1 tbsp..)
- Olive oil (3 tbsp..)
- Veggie broth (4 cups)
- Coconut milk (1 can)
- Thyme (1 tsp)

Method

- In a large pot, sauté onions and garlic using olive oil
- Add carrots & potatoes, thyme & broth
- Bring to a boil (until veggies are soft)
- Lower heat and simmer for 30 minutes
- Using an immersion blender (or bender) blend
- Pour back in pot (if using a regular blender)
- Add coconut milk & stir
- Simmer
- Add salt, pepper, smoked paprika

Use a little paprika for garnish

Callaloo & Okra Soup

(Grenadian)

Ingredients

- Callaloo (6 cups)
- Okra (4-5 sliced)
- Sweet Potatoes (1 ½ cups diced)
- Butternut Squash (1 ½ cups diced)
- Onion (1 small diced)
- Garlic (4 cloves minced)
- Scotch Bonnet pepper (sliced)
- Scallion (3 chopped)
- Thyme (½ tbsp..)
- Himalayan Pink salt (1 tsp)
- Black pepper (¼ tsp)
- Veggie stock (2 cups)
- Coconut Milk (2 cups)
- Coconut Oil (2 tbsp..)

Method

- On medium heat using coconut oil, sauté onion, scallion, and garlic until soft (1-2 minutes)
- Add potatoes, squash, okra & scallion stirring frequently for 5 minutes
- Add scotch bonnet pepper, thyme, black pepper, salt & stir
- Stir and Callaloo & simmer
- Add Coconut milk and veggie stock, reduce to low
- Cover pot and allow to reduce. Stir often
- After desired thickness, use immersion blender (or regular blender) to make it smooth

if using regular blender, return to pot and stir
use scotch bonnet pepper, thyme, spice, or scallion for garnish

Southwest Quinoa Soup

(American/Mexican)

Ingredients (3-4 servings)

- Black beans (15.5 oz. can rinsed and drained)
- Frozen Corn (8 oz.)
- Green Onion (1/3 cup chopped)
- Tomatoes (1 cup chopped)
- Cilantro (¼ cup chopped)
- Lime (Juice of 3)
- Cumin (3 tsp)
- Jalapenos (1 deseeded and chopped)
- Quinoa (1 ½ cups cooked)
- Olive Oil (1 tbsp..)
- Veggie Broth (40 0z)
- Salt (to taste)
- Onion Powder (½ tbsp..)
- Chili Powder (1 tbsp..)
- Garlic Powder (½ tbsp..)

Method

- In a large pot on medium high heat using olive oil, cook beans, corn and Jalapeno for 5 minutes stirring frequently
- Add all dry ingredients and stir
- Add Quinoa & Veggie broth and stir
- Reduce heat to low and simmer for 8-10 minutes
- Add lime juice, green onion, cilantro, tomatoes. Stir and simmer 3-5 minutes more

Garnish w/ cilantro

Creamy Tomato Basil Soup

(American)

Ingredients (4-6 servings)

- Tomatoes (8 cups chopped)
- Basil (4 oz.)
- Onion (1 medium chopped)
- Kosher Salt (to taste)
- Pepper (to taste)
- Almond milk (½ cup)
- Olive oil (1 tbsp..)

Method

- In a pot over medium heat, add oil and sauté onion and garlic with a pinch of salt
- Add tomatoes and stir 3-5 minutes
- Add milk and cook 3 more minutes
- Pour in a blender adding Basil and blend until smooth
- Return to pot adjusting salt & pepper to taste

use basil for garnish

SALADS

- THAI Cucumber Salad (Thai)
- Garden Salad Tossed in apple cider Vinaigrette (American)
- Pasta Salad (Mediterranean)

Thai Cucumber Salad

(Thai)

Ingredients (3-5 servings)

- English Cucumber (peeled sliced diagonally then across)
- Red Onion (1 large sliced thin)
- Agave Nectar (3 tbsp..)
- Sea salt (to taste)
- Lime Juice (Juice of 1 lime)
- Chopped Cashews (½ cup)
- Cayenne Pepper (1 tbsp..)
- Apple Cider Vinegar (¼ cup)
- Garlic Cloves (2 grated very fine)
- Sesame Oil (2 tbsp..)

Method

- Whisk together agave nectar, Lime juice, Sesame oil, Cayenne pepper, Garlic, Apple cider vinegar
- In a separate bowl, toss together cucumbers, onions and cashews
- Coat salad with dressing and toss
- Add a small amount of salt to taste

Garden Salad Tossed in an Apple Cider Vinaigrette

(American)

Ingredients (6 Servings)

- Roman Lettuce (3 hearts chopped)
- English Cucumber (Peeled, Deseeded & Diced)
- Tomatoes (3 Roma Diced)
- Carrots (2 Peeled & Shredded)
- Red Onion (1 chopped)
- Apple Cider Vinaigrette Dressing (Recipe in last section)

Method

- Coat with Salad dressing and toss

Pasta Salad

(Mediterranean)

Ingredients (6-8 servings)

- Arugula (Handful)
- Parsley (Handful)
- Basil (1 Handful)
- Olive Oil (3 tbsp..)
- Lemon (Juice of ½)
- Cherry tomatoes (12 cut in halves)
- Garlic Powder (2tsp)
- Sea Salt (to taste)
- Ground Black Pepper (to taste)
- Penne Pasta (1 box)
- Black olives (1 cup sliced)

Method

- Boil pasta " AL Dente ", drain, mix with 1 tbsp.. of olive oil
- After cooled, place in a big bowl and mix all ingredients together well
- Allow to sit 20-30 minutes before serving

ENTRÉES

African Peanut Stew (African)
Mushroom Stroganoff (Russian)
Yellow Mango Curry (Thai)
Brown Stew Cauliflower (Jamaican)
Palak Mushroom Sabzi (Indian)
Trini Chana Aloo (Trinidadian)
Stir Fry Vegetables with Garlic Sauce (Chinese)
Red Lentil Dahl (Indian)
Pizza (Italian)
Black Bean Burger w/ Sweet Chili Sauce (American)
Mac and Cheese (American)

African Peanut Stew

African Peanut Stew

(African)

Ingredients (4-6 servings)

- Olive Oil (3 tbsp..)
- Scallion (1 cup chopped)
- Yellow Onion (½ cup chopped)
- Garlic (4 cloves minced)
- Ginger (1 inch crushed)
- Cloves (5-7)
- Cinnamon (1 tsp)
- Nutmeg (A dash or 2)
- Cumin (1 tbsp..)

- Crushed Chili Peppers (A pinch)
- Cayenne Powder (2 tsp)
- Sea salt (to taste)
- Vegetable Broth (4 cups)
- Roasted Tomatoes (28 oz.)
- Chunky Peanut Butter (½ cup)
- Sweet Potatoes (3 cut in cubes)
- Kale, Spinach, or Collard Greens (3 cups)

* Cilantro and/or Peanuts for Garnish*

Method

- Heat oil in pot (medium to medium high heat)
- Stir in ginger, garlic, onion until soft and onions are translucent (about 3 minutes)
- Add all dry seasonings & cloves then stir
- Pour in Veggie stock and boil
- Reduce heat to low and cover allowing 20 minutes to simmer
- Stir in greens of choice, tomatoes, and peanut butter
- Cover & Stir occasionally for about 20-30 minutes
- Adjust salt to taste
- Use Cilantro & Peanuts to garnish

Mushroom Stroganoff

(Russian)

Ingredients (4-6 Servings)

- Olive oil (3 tbsp..)
- Shallots (2 minced)
- Garlic cloves (5 pressed)
- Baby Portabella Mushrooms (2 cups sliced)
- Egg Free Pasta (1 box)
- Sea salt (to taste)
- White Pepper (to taste)
- Garbanzo Bean Flour (1 tbsp..)
- Almond Milk (1 ½ cup)
- Vegetable broth (¾ cups)

Method

- Boil pasta
- Sauté garlic, shallots and mushrooms in sauté pan on medium heat
- Add flour and stir
- Add milk and broth
- Simmer and stir until thick and creamy
- Add sea salt and white pepper to taste
- Serve over cooked and drained pasta

Garnish with parsley, scallion, etc.

Red curry mango

Red Mango Curry

(Thai)

Ingredients

- Coconut oil (2 tbsp..)
- Mangos (2 ripe & diced)
- Red bell pepper
- Serrano pepper (1 sliced with no stem and seeded)
- Garlic (3 cloves minced)
- Shallots (1 minced)
- Red curry paste (2 tbsp..)
- Coconut Sugar (5 tbsp..)
- Coconut milk (28 oz.)
- Juice of (½ lime)
- Soy sauce (3 tsp)
- Turmeric (2 tbsp..)

Lime, pepper, herb for Garnish

Method

- Coconut oil on medium heat and add garlic, shallots, ginger, and serrano pepper
- Add curry paste, turmeric, coconut sugar and stir for a minute or 2
- Add coconut milk and soy sauce and simmer on medium-low for about 10 minutes stirring 2 or 3 times in between
- Add peeled ripe mango, red pepper, and lime juice. Stir and simmer (still on medium-low) for 5 minutes

Garnish with lime, pepper, or fresh herbs

Brown Stew Cauliflower

Brown Stew Cauliflower

(Jamaica)

Ingredients (4 servings)

- Cauliflower (1 head)
- Carrot (1 large sliced)
- Red bell pepper (¼ sliced)
- Green bell pepper (¼ sliced)
- Onion (medium ¼ sliced)
- Garlic (2 cloves minced)

- Scotch bonnet / Habanero pepper (½ tsp chopped)
- Sea salt (2 tsp)
- Ground black pepper (1 tsp)
- Ground all spice (1 tsp)
- Thyme (1 tbsp.. fresh or dried)

- Brown sugar (2 tbsp..)
- Browning (1 tbsp..)
- Soy sauce (2 tbsp..)
- Ketchup (3 tbsp..)
- Veggie stock or water (3 cups)
- Vegetable oil (3 tbsp..)

Garnish w/ one fresh thyme spring

Method

- Cut cauliflower into flat steaks
- Sprinkle all spice, salt, pepper and toss

- And Scotch bonnet/Habanero pepper, thyme carrots, onion, bell peppers, garlic, and toss again
- Pour browning into mixture, mix again

mixture can be covered to sit & marinate or cooked right away. However, most dishes taste better when all spices and flavoring sit and marry for a couple hours or longer

- Separate cauliflower from other ingredients
- Heat pot of oil on medium high heat
- Once hot, place pieces of cauliflower in pan giving space in between each one (overcrowding the pan will cause too much moisture preventing cauliflower from frying/browning properly)
- Brown each side 4-5 minutes
- Placed the finished fried/browned pieces of cauliflower on a separate dish as you continue to brown all pieces

- When finished, reduce heat and add remaining ingredients from mixture and sauté for 5 minutes
- Add ketchup and a pinch or two of both salt & pepper. Stir and cook for one minute.
- Turn heat back up to medium high heat, now adding veggie stock or water.
- Add and stir sugar, soy sauce, and remainder of salt & pepper
- Simmer (without pot cover) for 10 minutes
- Sir & cover
- Reduce heat to low and cook 5 minutes more

Garnish with thyme sprigs

Palak Mushroom Sabzi

(Indian)

Ingredients (3-5 servings)

- Fresh spinach (10 oz. chopped)
- White button mushroom (8 oz. sliced)
- Roma tomatoes (2 diced)
- Onion (1 large pureed)
- Garlic cloves (5 minced)
- Ginger (½ inched crushed)
- Green Chilies (2 sliced & seeded)
- Sea salt (to taste)

- Black pepper (1 tbsp..)
- Cardamom Powder (2 tsp)
- Garam Masala (2 tsp)
- Olive oil (5 tsp)
- Creamy coconut milk (4 oz.)
- Lemon (½ tbsp.. from juice)
- Water (For boiling)

Method

- Boil water and add spinach (don't boil too long, about 1 minute or less, until bright green)
- Blanch spinach (Plunge in ice water after boil)
- In blender, puree spinach and allow to sit in blender for a little while.
- Boil water again using less than 1 tsp of salt and lemon juice. Add mushrooms and boil for 5 minutes.
- Drain mushrooms.
- Heat oil in pain and sauté mushrooms.
- Add onion puree, tomato & garlic and sauté as well.
- Add all dry ingredients & stir.
- Add spinach puree and salt to taste and simmer.
- Add cold creamy coconut milk after 10 minutes.

If coconut milk is not creamy enough before adding to the pan, simmer first and let cool then add to pan *peppers for garnish*

Trini Chana Aloo

(Trinidad)

Ingredients (4-5 servings)

- Chickpeas (dried 4 cups)
- Scotch bonnet peppers/Habanero (1 seeded and minced)
- Garlic (5 cloves minced)
- Onion (1 small/medium)
- Turmeric (2 tsp)
- Cumin (1 tsp)

- Curry powder (2 tbsp..)
- Sea salt (to taste)
- Cilantro (2 tbsp..) *optional*
- Potatoes (2 medium diced)
- Olive oil (2 tbsp..)
- Water

Cilantro for garnish

Method

- Soak dried chickpeas in water overnight
- Boil chickpeas for 2 hours adding potatoes into boil for the last 20 minutes
- Drain chickpeas and potatoes, set aside excess water
- Using the same pot, dry out any water left and heat oil over medium heat
- Sauté onions until translucent (about 4 or 5 minutes)
- Add Scotch bonnet/Habanero peppers and garlic and stir for a couple minutes
- Add all dry ingredients and stir for 20-30 seconds
- Add 1 cup of the excess water that was set aside from draining peas and potatoes and stir, simmer for 5 minutes
- Add chickpeas and potatoes, and more water if needed (between ¼ cup to ½ cup, salt to taste, stir and simmer uncovered for 15-20 minutes stirring in between
- Reduce heat to low, cover pot and allow to cook 3-5 minutes longer
- Add and stir in cilantro if desired

Garnish with cilantro

Stir fry vegetables with garlic sauce

Stir Fry Vegetables w/ Garlic Sauce

(Chinese)

Ingredients (3-4 servings)

- Carrots (1 large & cut diagonally)
- Onion (½ large & sliced)
- Snow peas (1 cup)
- Red bell pepper (½ sliced)
- Broccoli (2 cups)
- Sesame oil (2 tablespoons)
- Sea salt (1 tsp)
- Toasted sesame seeds
- Garlic sauce (recipe in last section)

Toasted sesame seeds for garnish

Method

- Heat oil in wok on medium high heat
- Add onions and carrots and stir fry for 2-3 minutes
- Add snow peas, red pepper, broccoli & salt
- Stir fry for 5 minutes more
- Toss in 2 tbsp.. of garlic sauce and sesame seeds if desired
- Pour more sauce on vegetables if desired

Garnish w/ sesame seeds

Red Dahl

Red Dahl

(Indian)

Ingredients (6 servings)

- Red lentils (1 ½ cups rinsed thoroughly & drain)
- Blended together making a paste like mixture
    - Turmeric (2 tbsp..)
    - Ginger (1 inch)
    - Garlic (3 cloves
- Mustard seeds (2 tsp)
- Cumin (2 tsp)
- Cinnamon (2 tsp)
- Black pepper (1 tsp)
- Sea salt or pink Himalayan (2 tsp)
- Garam Masala (2 tsp)
- Olive oil (2 tbsp..)
- Cilantro (1 tsp)

Cilantro chopped as garnish

Method

- Heat oil in pot on medium high heat
- Fry mustard seeds until it starts to pop, then add the ginger, garlic, turmeric mixture & stir for 15 seconds
- Add drained lentils and stir fry for 1 minute
- Add 2 ¼ cups of water, cover pot and simmer for 15 minutes stirring a few times in between
- Add remainder of dry spices and cilantro
- Reduce heat to low, stir, cover, simmer for 5 minutes
- Garnish with cilantro

Pizza

Pizza
(Italian)

Ingredients (2 servings)

- Tomato paste
- Roma Tomato (1 sliced thin)
- Fresh Basil (5 or 6 leaves)
- Chickpea Flour (1 cup sifted)
- Garlic Powder (1 tbsp..)
- Sea salt (2 tbsp..)
- Water (1 ½ cup)
- Olive oil (2 tsp)
- Nutritional Yeast (Optional to top pizza)

Method

- Place oven on 355 °F
- In a bowl, mix flour, water, garlic powder, salt and stir
- Stir in olive oil well
- On a baking sheet, top with parchment paper, pour mixture slowly and evenly
- Using a large spoon, spread in a circular motion
- Bake for 15 minutes
- Spread tomato paste evenly, add sliced tomatoes and place in oven for another 10 minutes
- Top with nutritional yeast and basil (if desired)

Black Bean Burger w/ Sweet Chili Sauce

(American)

Ingredients (3-5 servings)

- Black beans (2 cans rinsed & drained)
- Carrots (2 shredded)
- Garlic Powder (1tsp)
- Red onion (2 or 3 slices)
- Cumin (1 tsp)
- Cayenne Pepper (½ tsp)
- Sea salt (1 tsp)
- Black Pepper (1 tsp)
- Coriander (½ tsp)

- Chili Powder (1 tsp)
- Onion Powder (1 tsp)
- Olive oil (3 tbsp..)
- Soy sauce (2 tsp)
- Quick Oats (½ cup)
- Sweet Chili Sauce (recipe in last section)
- Avocado (2 or 3 slices)
- Arugula (as needed for burger)
- Hamburger Buns / Brioche Buns

Method

- Using a potato masher, in a mixing bowl, mash black beans for 2 to 3 minutes
- In the same bowl, add all ingredients except: buns, arugula, red onion, avocado, and sweet chili sauce
- Mix well
- Form into patties and put on parchment paper on tray and freeze for 20-30 minutes
- On medium high heat, heat oil and fry patties for 2 to 3 minutes on each side
- Place patty on bun, then avocado, red onions, desired amount of sweet chili sauce and arugula

Enjoy with Potato Wedges

Mac & Cheese

(American)

Ingredients (6-8 servings)

- Nutritional yeast (½ cup)
- Garlic powder (½ tbsp..)
- Sea salt (1 tbsp..)
- Turmeric (1 tsp)
- Lemon Juice (4 tbsp..)
- Cashews (1 ½ cups soaked in hot water)
- Water (1 cup)
- Elbow pasta (1 box/16 oz.)

Method

- - Boil pasta
- - Sit cashews in hot boiled water for about 5 minutes
- - In a blender, add soaked cashews, turmeric, lemon juice, salt, garlic powder, and water and blend until very smooth
- - When pasta has finished boiling, drain and return to the pot
- - Stir in "cheese" and let settle a few minutes before serving

green onion for garnish

Desserts

- Peanut Butter Chocolate-Banana Ice cream, (American)
- Mbatata / Sweet Potato Cookies (African)
- Soapaipillas (Chilean)

Peanut Butter Chocolate-Banana Ice Cream

(American)

Ingredients (2-3 servings)

- Bananas (5 ripe, sliced, frozen overnight)
- Peanut butter (2 tbsp..)
- Cocoa / Cacao Powder (2 tbsp.)

Method

- Give bananas about 2 minutes before placing in a processor and blending for 45 seconds
- Add Cocoa / Cocoa powder & Peanut butter
- Blend for 1 minute until smooth

Mbatata Cookies

(African)

Ingredients (1 dozen)

- Sweet potatoes (2 peeled & chopped)
- Apple Sauce (¼ cup)
- All purpose Flour (1 ¼ cup)
- Vegan Butter (4 tbsp. softened)
- Baking powder (2 tsp)
- Cinnamon (2 tsp)
- Raisins (½ cup)
- Brown sugar (½ cup)
- Salt (½ tsp)

Method

- Preheat Oven to 375°
- Boil potatoes & Mash with fork
- In a mixer, first combine butter and mashed potatoes for one minute
- Slowly add remainder of ingredients one at a time for 3 minutes
- Using a spoon or ice cream scooper, place one by one on a parchment paper topped cookie sheet and be sure to give about 1 ½ - 2 inches of space between each drop
- Bake for 18-20 minutes

Soapaipillas

(Chilean)

Ingredients (15 Count)

- Whole wheat flour (2 cups)
- Baking Powder (1 tsp)
- Salt (1 tsp)
- Butternut Squash (2 cups chopped)
- Vegetable Oil (enough for frying)
- Vegan Butter (2 tbsp..)

Method

- Boil squash until very soft and drain
- Combine softened vegan butter with squash and mix in a bowl
- Combine flour and mix again
- Knead into a big ball, then on a flat surface on parchment paper, press down flat
- Using a rolling pin, roll out
- Using a cookie cutter or a cup, cut out circles and poke holes in each one using a fork
- Fry each side on medium heat for a minute to 90 seconds each. Do not burn.

Eat with Salsa (recipe in last section) for a savory taste, use Agave syrup for a sweet taste

Accompaniments

- Mango Pineapple Chutney (Indian)
- Garlic Sauce (Chinese)
- Sweet Chili Sauce (Thai)
- Salsa (Mexican)
- Zesty Lime Sauce (Bahamian)
- Apple Cider Vinaigrette (American)

Mango Pineapple Chutney

(Indian)

Ingredients (4+ servings)

- Pineapple (1 cup diced)
- Mango (1 cup diced)
- Black mustard seeds (¼ tsp)
- Sugar (turbinado or brown) (1 ½ tbsp.. to taste)
- Cumin (1 tsp)
- Vinegar (½ tsp)
- Water (¼ cup)
- Salt (to taste)
- Red Chili Flakes (1 ½ tsp)
- Olive oil (1 tbsp.)

Method

- In a pan, heat oil on medium heat
- Add mustard seed and stir for a few seconds
- Add pineapples, mangoes, salt, water, vinegar and mix
- Add sugar, cover pot, cook for 5 minutes
- Stir & add more sugar and salt if desired
- Add cumin and chili flakes, stir, cover and cook for 5 more minutes

Garlic Sauce

(Chinese)

Ingredients (4 servings)

- Soy sauce (4 tbsp..)
- Chili sauce (1 tsp)
- Sesame oil (1 tsp)
- Corn Starch (2 tsp)
- Water (2 tbsp..)
- Peanut oil (1 tbsp..)
- Chinese rice wine / Rice Vinegar (3 tsp)
- Sugar "turbinado" (1 ¼ tbsp..)
- Garlic (4 cloves chopped)

Method

- Combine Soy sauce, rice vinegar, sugar, chili sauce, sesame oil in a small bowl and stir
- In another bowl, dissolve cornstarch in water
- Heat oil in saucepan over medium heat, add garlic & stir for 30 seconds
- Stir sauce again and add to saucepan
- Bring to a boil and stir for 1 minute
- Add cornstarch and water mixture to the pan and stir to desired thickness

Sweet Chili Sauce

(Thai)

Ingredients (4 servings)

- Sambal Oelek (1 ½ tbsp.)
- Rice wine (¼ cup)
- Sugar (½ cup) *turbinado sugar*
- Water (¼ cup) + (1 tbsp.)
- Cornstarch (½ tbsp.)

Method

- Over medium heat, add sugar, Rice wine, Sambal Oelek, ¼ cup of water in a sauce pot
- Stir ingredients until sugar dissolves
- In a stir cornstarch and 1 tbsp. of water together
- When cornstarch and water mixture is dissolved, add in the pot
- Stir and simmer until sauce thickens

Salsa

(Mexican)

Ingredients (10 servings)

- Roma tomatoes (2 ½ cups diced)
- Fresh cilantro (4 tbsp.)
- White Onion (½ cup diced)
- Lime juice (1 tbsp. from fresh lime)
- Sea salt (to taste)
- Garlic (2 cloves minced)
- Jalapeños (3 tsp deseeded & minced)

Method

- Combine all ingredients stirring together well.

Zesty Lime Fritter Sauce

(Bahamian)

Ingredients (3-6)

- Coconut milk (½ cup) (canned)
- Lime (juice of ½)
- Ketchup (2 tbsp.)
- Salt (to taste)
- Hot sauce (1 tbsp.)

Method

- In a non-stick sauce pan on medium heat, add coconut milk and simmer (uncovered) for 5 minutes stirring in between
- Add lime juice, stir in, simmer uncovered for another minute
- Remove from fire, allow to thicken, stir, ready for serving

never use top and cover while cooking

Apple Cider Vinaigrette

(American)

Ingredients

- Apple Cider Vinegar (¼ cup)
- Garlic (1 clove minced)
- Shallots (½ minced)
- Agave nectar (2 tbsp.)
- Lemon juice (2 tbsp. fresh squeezed)
- Olive oil (1/3 cup)
- Salt (to taste)
- Pepper (to taste)

Method

- In a large bowl, whisk garlic, shallots, salt, pepper, lemon juice, agave nectar, olive oil for 30 seconds
- Add apple cider and whisk for one minute

Printed in the United States
By Bookmasters